BETTER ICE SKATING
for Boys and Girls

George Sullivan

DODD, MEAD & COMPANY · NEW YORK

Many people helped the author in making this book possible. Special thanks are offered the following: Instructor Archie Walker, Le Petit Ice Skating Studio, New York City, for his technical assistance; Jim Reed, Rockefeller Center, Inc., for granting permission to use the ice skating rink there; and photographer Michel Le Grou, Wagner-International Photos, Inc. The author is also grateful to Ruth Jackson, U.S. Figure Skating Association; Barbara Graham, Canadian Figure Skating Association; Lawrence Ralston, Amateur Skating Union of the U.S.; John Hurdis, Canadian Amateur Speed Skating Association; Jean Michel Le Grou, Larry LaMontagne, Tommy Columbo, and Tim Sullivan.

PICTURE CREDITS

Amateur Skating Union of the United States, 58 (left); Canadian Amateur Speed Skating Association, 57; Canadian Amateur Speed Skating Association (Brian Thususka), 58 (right), 59, 60; Danskin Inc., 14 (right); New York Public Library, 62; Polar Sport, 15; Riedell Shoes, Inc., 9 (left); Strauss Skates, Inc., 9 (right); George Sullivan, 10, 19, 20, 26, 55, 56; Wagner-International Photos, 6, 7 (right), 12, 14 (left), 16, 17, 18, 21, 22, 23, 25, 27, 28, 29, 30, 32 33, 35, 36, 38, 39, 40, 41, 42, 43, 44, 45, 46, 47, 48, 50, 54; Margaret Williamson, 2, 8, 51, 52.

Frontispiece: **Photo by Margaret Williamson**

Copyright © 1976 by George Sullivan
All rights reserved
No part of this book may be reproduced in any form without permission in writing from the publisher
Distributed in Canada by
McClelland and Stewart Limited, Toronto
Manufactured in the United States of America

3 4 5 6 7 8 9 10

Library of Congress Cataloging in Publication Data

Sullivan, George, 1927–
    Better ice skating for boys and girls.

    SUMMARY: Discusses basic and advanced ice skating skills, equipment, and three styles of skating; competitive figure, power, and speed skating.
    1. Skating—Juvenile literature. [1. Ice skating] I. Title.
GV849.S85   796.9'1   76-12425
ISBN 0-396-07339-5
ISBN 0-396-08475-3 (pbk.)

Books in This Series

Better Baseball for Boys
Better Basketball for Boys
Better Basketball for Girls
Better Bicycling for Boys and Girls
Better Boxing for Boys
Better Cross-Country Running for Boys and Girls
Better Field Events for Girls
Better Field Hockey for Girls
Better Football for Boys
Better Gymnastics for Girls
Better Horseback Riding for Boys and Girls
Better Ice Skating for Boys and Girls
Better Karate for Boys
Better Kite Flying for Boys and Girls
Better Roller Skating for Boys and Girls
Better Skateboarding for Boys and Girls
Better Soccer for Boys and Girls
Better Softball for Boys and Girls
Better Swimming for Boys and Girls
Better Synchronized Swimming for Girls
Better Tennis for Boys and Girls
Better Track for Girls
Better Volleyball for Girls
Better Weight Training for Boys

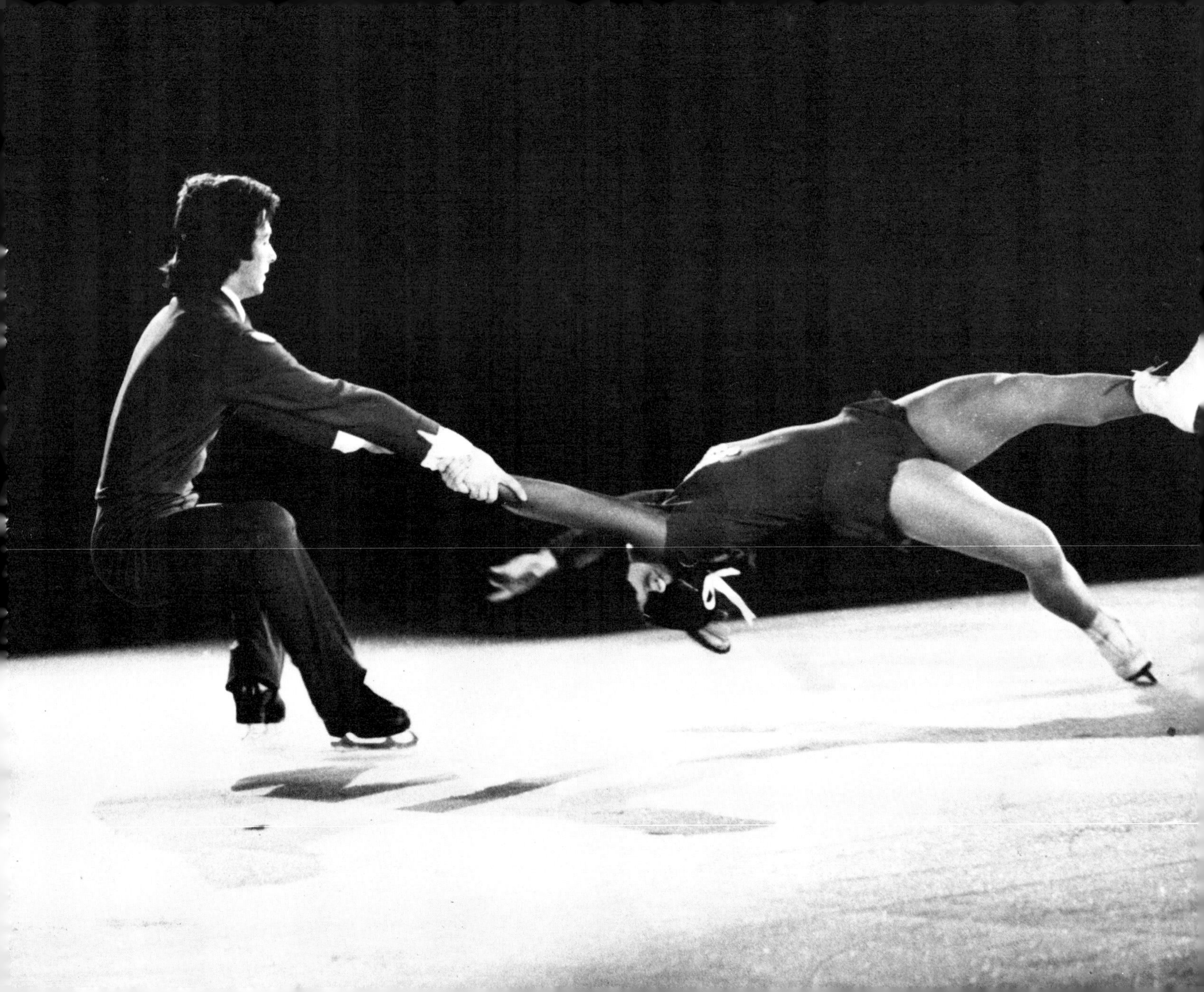

CONTENTS

Introduction	6	Two-Foot Spin	40
Equipment	9	Bunny Hop	43
First Time on the Ice	16	Forward Spiral	44
Sculling	19	Waltz Jump	46
Stroking	21	Pivots	48
T-Stop	24	The Figure 8	49
Hockey Stop	26	Competitive Figure Skating	51
Skating Backward	27	Power Skating	54
Backward Stopping	29	Speed Skating	57
Skating Edges	31	Some History	61
Crossovers	35	Glossary	64
The Three-Turn	37		

INTRODUCTION

Ice skating, known for hundreds of years, is more popular today than ever before. Rinks are crowded day and night. Equipment sales are at record levels. Interest in skating competition has never been greater.

A primary reason for the sport's popularity is that there is a type of skating to suit every taste. First, there's figure skating. Figure skating includes the execution of the figures themselves, which consist of certain designs etched upon the ice, all of which are based on the figure 8.

Figure skating also refers to free skating. Free skating consists of jumps, spins, spirals, and other "free" movements performed to music, and similar to what one sees in ice shows. It is these two branches of figure skating upon which this book concentrates.

Figure skating also includes pair skating and ice dancing. Pair skating is free skating—various lifts and spins and other free movements—executed by two skaters in unison. Ice dancing is ballroom dancing to music on the ice.

Besides figure skating in all of its forms, there are two other types of skating: power skating and speed skating.

Power skating is for playing ice hockey. It's different from figure skating in that there's effort to put greater power into each thrust and use longer strides. Watch Bobby Orr of the Boston Bruins. He's one

Taking lessons assures that you'll make rapid progress.

of the great power skaters of all time.

Speed skating is just what the term implies. It involves competing against another skater or a stopwatch at speeds of from 25 to 30 miles an hour, which is about the fastest speed a human can achieve, using his two feet.

No matter what type of skating you plan to pursue, you should take lessons. Most rinks offer both private and group instruction. One can learn at a faster rate through individual instruction, but the cost is considerably greater than in the case of group instruction.

You also have to skate frequently in order to be able to make steady improvement. Most instruction specialists recommend two or three practice sessions a week.

If your specialty is figure skating, you'll want to become a member of the United States Figure Skating Association (Sears Crescent, Suite 500, City Hall Plaza, Boston, Massachusetts 02108). The USFSA describes itself as "the governing body for

Emblems of United States Figure Skating Association and Canadian Figure Skating Association.

Badges indicate skater's progress.

figure skating on ice in the United States." In Canada a similar organization is the Canadian Figure Skating Association (333 River Road, Ottawa, Canada K1L 8B9).

Individual figure skaters become registered with the USFSA by joining a skating club that holds membership in the organization. There are about 200 such clubs in the United States (and more than 900 in Canada). Most clubs rent public rinks for skating sessions, but some own their own rinks. Club programs usually include instruction on all levels. To get information on skating clubs in your area, contact the manager of a local skating rink.

Through its member clubs, the USFSA provides a wide-ranging program to encourage the development of figure skating skills. So that you, as a beginner, can measure your progress, the USFSA offers a series of "Basic Tests." These span several levels, including "Beginner," "Novice," "Intermediate," and

Dorothy Hamill (left) and Janet Lynn were American figure skating champions in recent years.

"Advanced." Whenever you pass a test, you earn a colorful embroidered badge.

The USFSA is more noted, of course, for the competition it conducts for boys and girls, men and women, on regional, sectional, and national levels. The organization, through its membership in the International Skating Union, sends its national champions to the annual World Figure Skating Championships, and also to the Olympic Winter Games.

While international competition in recent years has frequently been dominated by Russian skaters, the United States and Canada have not fared badly. Dorothy Hamill of the United States won the World Figure Skating Championship in 1976. Canada's Karen Magnussen was the world's titlist in 1973. Tim Wood of the United States was the men's champion in 1970.

Whether you're planning to be a figure skater, a speed skater, or to play hockey, it's vital that you begin by getting the right equipment. That subject is covered in the next section.

EQUIPMENT

One of the best things about skating is that it requires little in the way of equipment. Aside from what clothing you might purchase, about all you need is the skates themselves and a pair of skate guards to protect the blades.

In your very first sessions on the ice, you may want to use rental equipment, that is, skates provided by the rink management for a small fee. It's a good idea to use rental skates until you've decided to become serious about the sport.

There are three different types of skates, each designed for a particular type of skating. There's the figure skate, the speed skate (sometimes called the racing skate), and the hockey skate.

All three types are the same in that each consists of a shoe with a bladelike metal runner fixed to the sole. In other words, there are two distinct parts—the shoe, properly called the boot, and the runner, or blade.

The figure skate is the type that is most widely used. It's the skate you'll want to buy for recreational skating, for gliding about the rink for a few hours each week with your friends. It's also the skate to use for free-style skating or the tracing of geometrical designs—figures—on the ice.

The figure skate is characterized by high-topped leather boots, which rise to a point just below calf level. The curved steel blade, about one-eighth of an inch in width, extends approximately an inch

Skate boot . . .

. . . and blade.

beyond the toe in front, and about two inches behind the heel in back. At the front of the blade, there's a series of teeth, called toe picks or toe rakes, which are used in executing certain spins and jumps.

You can buy the boots and blades separately or in pre-matched sets, that is, the blade will already have been mounted to the boot. Since some firms specialize in the manufacture of boots and others in blades, the best equipment is bought separately.

Hockey skate is of tubular construction, has no toe picks.

After you've made your purchase, the dealer mounts the blades to the boots for you.

The hockey skate features a low-cut boot with extra padding around the ankle, hard toe caps, and molded heel counters. The lightweight blade has no teeth in front, and is fitted with a tendon guard at the heel end. This is to prevent the blade end of one skate from injuring the Achilles' tendon of the other foot.

The speed skate is recognized by its long, thin blade. The lightweight boot is low cut. The speed skate is designed for straight stroking, for achieving high speeds with the greatest possible efficiency.

There are also double-runner blades, which young children sometimes use. Instructors frown on the use of double-runners, saying that it is not possible to learn how to skate properly while using them. When the child switches to a single blade, he or she has to learn how to skate from the beginning. Double-runners are really non-skates. Steer clear of them.

When you purchase skates, have them fitted by an expert. This means dealing with a skate shop or with a professional instructor at a local rink, rather than at a department store or discount store.

BOOTS—Properly fitted boots are more important to good skating than any other single factor. They will impart both support and comfort. Boots begin in price at about $40 and range up to twice that amount.

The higher the quality of the boots, the more

success you are likely to have with them. The boot's counter is very important. The counter is the stiff piece of leather that supports the instep and holds the heel in place.

On the instep side of the foot, the counter should be long enough and strong enough to push the foot into an upright position and hold it there. In addition, the counter should cup the heel, keeping it firmly in place.

Examine the upper of each boot. The upper is that part of the boot above the sole. It must be firm enough to hold the foot in place and protect it, but also have the flexibility to permit you to move and bend the ankle. It should not be so high at the back of the foot that it covers the lower calf muscles.

The boot sole should be so firm that it is extremely difficult or virtually impossible for you to bend the sole with your hands. The insole, the extra strip of material inside the boot, should be made of high quality leather.

The tongue of the boot should have sufficient padding so as to protect the instep from the pull of the laces. The hooks and eyelets should be firmly anchored.

As for color, it's usual for boys to wear black boots, and girls to wear white.

When having boots fitted, wear the same type of socks you plan to wear when skating. These can be socks of normal thickness. They don't have to be particularly heavy; they don't have to be wool. Girls often wear tights. Because tights are thin, the boots fit the feet better.

Your regular shoe size means little when you're being fitted for boots. Use it only as a starting point.

Snugness is what you want to strive for. One method of assuring a snug fit is to begin by making a tracing of one foot. Place the foot on a piece of blank paper and trace around it with a pencil. Hold the pencil upright.

Then pull out the innersole from a pair of boots that are of your approximate size. Place the heel of the innersole against the heel of the tracing. If the toe of the tracing extends beyond the toe of the innersole by ¼ to ⅜ of an inch, then the boots are likely to be of proper size for you.

Don't be too concerned about width. Quality boots can be ordered in different widths, and width can also be adjusted to some degree by the tightness of the lacing.

Once you're found a pair of boots you feel are the right size, lace them all the way to the top and stand erect. Each should feel snug beneath the ball of the foot, across the arch, and in the heel area. There should be no wrinkles in the leather from the toe area to the heel on either side, nor up the ankle.

Try this test: Hold the boot to the floor and try moving the heel up and down. If there is any more than the slightest bit of heel movement, the boot may be too big.

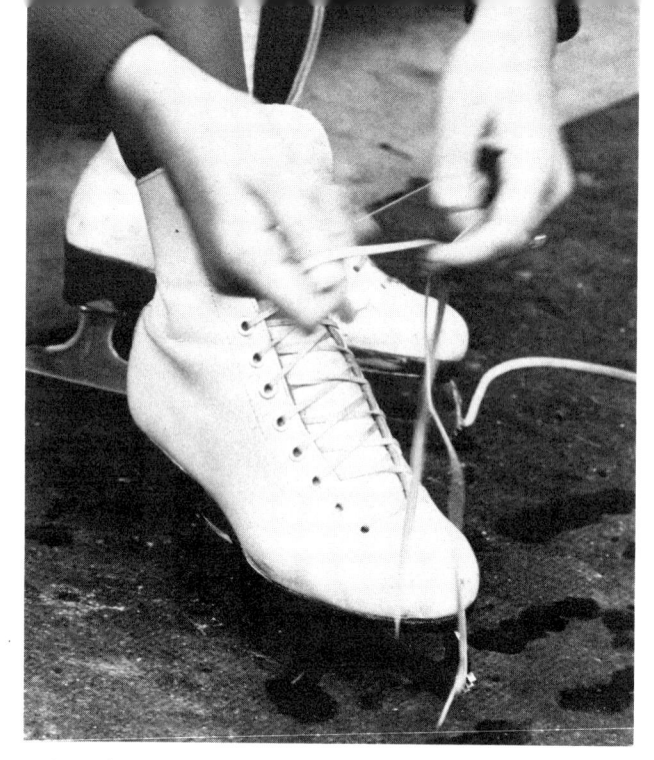

Lacing should be tightest over the instep.

You may experience some discomfort at the back of the ankle or at the side of the ankle bone, particularly if you have big ankle bones. But after a few skating sessions, the leather will begin to mold itself to the shape of your foot and the discomfort is likely to disappear.

The only place the boot need not be snug is in the toe area. When you stand erect, your toes should just touch the boot ends.

There are almost as many theories on how to lace skates as there are skaters. Many instructors advise lacing quite tightly up to the hooks, then finishing so as to impart a "just snug" feeling. This method keeps the foot firmly in the boot but gives the ankle some room to move.

Tie a double knot at the top. Tuck what remains of the laces between the tongue and the boot (not between the tongue and the leg; the movement of your ankle will cause the laces to fall out).

Laces are usually either cotton or nylon. Most skaters prefer nylon laces because they have some "give" to them.

BLADES—Blades range in price from about $15 to $100 and even beyond, depending upon the quality of the steel and the finish. Workmanship is also important. With a quality blade, the welds that join the heel and sole plates to the vertical members of the blade (called stanchions), are smooth and virtually undetectable.

Put a pair of skates together blade-to-blade, hold them up to the light, and you will see that each blade is gently curved from front to back. This curve is known as the radius. The amount of curvature in figure blades is about the same as that of a circle having a radius of six feet.

Racing blades are perfectly flat from one end to the other. Hockey blades are rather a compromise between the two extremes. Each of the blade ends is curved, but they are flat in the middle. The longer the flat, as the straight section is called, the greater speed and stability a player has, but he's less able to turn and cut. A defenseman may have a flat that measures four or five inches, while a forward's is shorter, only three or four inches.

How the blade is mounted to the boot is a critical matter. It should be mounted just inside the midline of the foot. To express it another way, the blade should be lined up with the space between the big toe and the second toe.

It's wrong to have the blade mounted exactly along the foot's midline, for this encourages the ankles to bend inward. You can end up practically walking on the sides of your boots. When this happens, it's normal for the victim to complain about being cursed with "weak ankles."

The blades should be mounted with screws, not rivets. Screws imply that the blades can be reset easily, in case they were mounted incorrectly the first time.

When you buy figure skates, the blade surface in contact with the ice will be "hollow ground." This means that instead of being flat, it has a concave surface, like the inner surface of a tennis or Ping-Pong ball. The result is two edges—an inside edge and an outside edge. If the blade were not hollow ground, it would slide sideways over the ice, and you would not be able to cut, turn, or stop.

The terms "inside edge" and "outside edge" will become especially meaningful to you once you begin doing figure work. The inside edge is the one along the arch-side of the foot. The outside edge is the one on the opposite side.

SKATE CARE—As you use your skates, the blade surfaces tend to flatten. To restore the hollow, the blades must be sharpened. This should be done by a professional skate sharpener.

How often you have your skates sharpened depends on how frequently you use them. The quality —the hardness—of the blade is also a factor. One professional skate sharpener recommends sharpening after every 15 sessions on the ice.

Protect your blades with skate guards, which are metal, vinyl, or wooden containers slightly larger than the blades themselves. Each guard is open down the center, permitting the blade to be inserted. A spring device holds the guard in place.

What the skate guards do is permit you to walk around without damaging the blades. The rubber matting that usually surrounds a commercial rink is put there so a skater can walk without using guards, but virtually any other surface, even carpet-

View of the blade from one end, showing hollow area between the two edges.

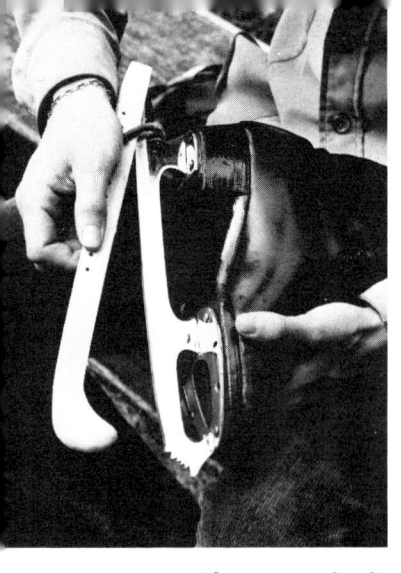

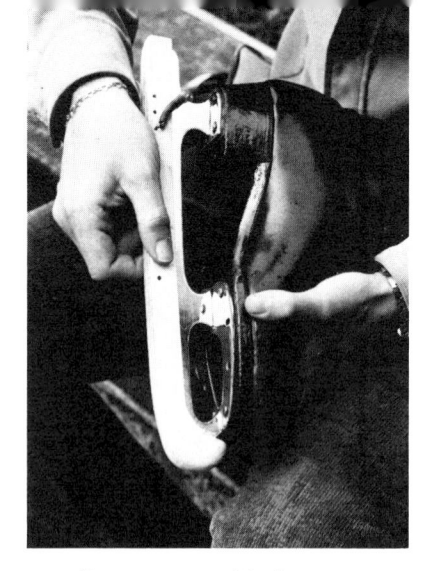

Skate guards slip on easily to protect blades.

ing, will work to dull the blades. Guards cost only $2 or $3.

Carry the skates to and from the rink in a tote bag. Vinyl or canvas bags that have a skate shape can be purchased for only a few dollars. Some skaters use airline tote bags.

Always carefully wipe the blades and boots with a dry towel after skating to prevent rust. Do this before you leave the rink.

You can buy any one of a variety of creams and lacquers to treat boot leather and waterproof it. But if you're careful about wiping down your skates after using them, such preparations aren't likely to be necessary.

From time to time, check the screws that hold

Skating outfits offer both comfort and style.

the blade to the boot. They may need tightening. Carry a small screwdriver in your tote bag to perform this job.

A loose screw not only presents the obvious hazard of a wobbly blade, but it also permits moisture to seep beneath the screw head. The rust that forms can damage the screw threads.

White boots, through day to day use, pick up black marks. You can wipe them away with nail polish remover.

CLOTHING—Clothing for beginning skaters should stress comfort. Girls skating at indoor rinks frequently wear outfits that include a short skating skirt with skating pants to match, stretch leotards, and a blouse or sweater.

In competitive figure skating, girls often wear dresses trimmed with lace or sequins. Boys wear custom-tailored jump suits in competition.

Stretch nylon warm-up uniforms, designed especially for skaters, are a recent innovation. The pants feature full-length zippers, so they can be zipped off quickly without having to remove the skates. The jacket is about the same length as the skating dress.

Never, in an effort to keep your feet warm, wear two pairs of socks. If you have room for more than one pair of socks, it indicates that the boots don't fit properly, and that your feet aren't being supported as they should be.

First warm-up suit for skaters

Hold onto the rail at first.

FIRST TIME ON THE ICE

On your first venture out onto the ice, your goal should be only to get the "feel" of your blades and learn to glide forward, even if it's only for a very short distance.

Use the rail or barrier that surrounds the rink as an aid. Take a firm grip and step carefully onto the ice.

Once there, don't attempt to move around. With one hand on the rail, simply stand on the ice. Keep your feet parallel and comfortably apart.

Because you may never have tried to stand on blades before, your ankles may have a tendency to bend inward. But strive to keep them straight. Little by little, you'll be able to acquire a feeling of stability.

Then, still holding onto the barrier, slide your blades forward and back a few times. All you're trying to do is get the feel of things.

Next, stand sideways to the barrier, and hold on with one hand. Bending both knees slightly, turn the right foot out so that it forms an angle of almost 90 degrees with the heel of the left skate. Release your hold on the rail.

Push firmly with the left blade; bring the skates together, and glide. Try it again. Push with the left blade, bring the skates together, and glide.

Now try pushing with the right foot. First, turn the left foot out so that it forms an angle of almost

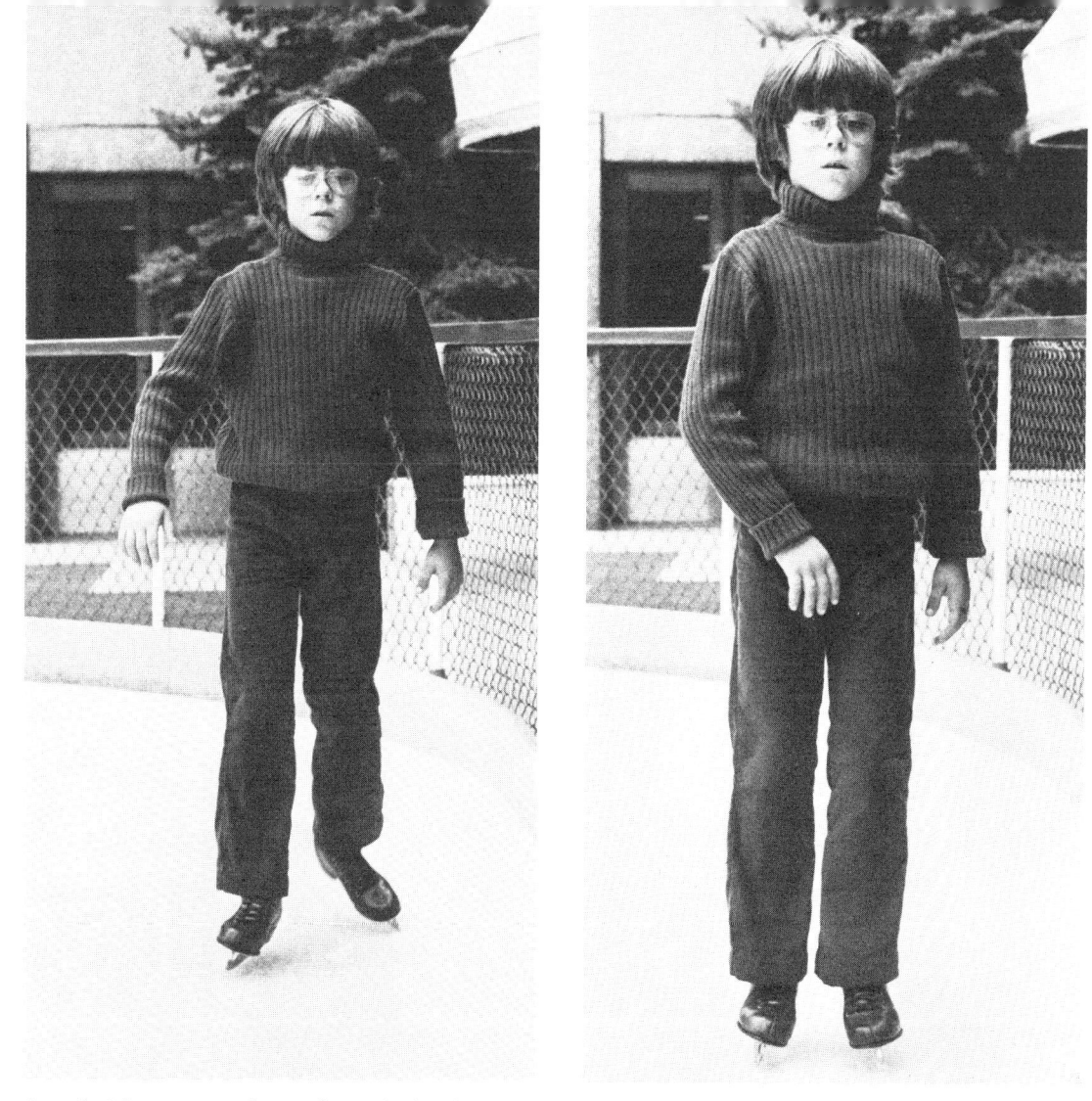

Stand sideways to the rail; push firmly, and glide. Keep trying until it's easy.

The snowplow stop

90 degrees with the heel of the right skate.

Push firmly with the right skate; bring the skates together, and glide.

Once you're able to glide, you can practice a simple method of stopping. It's called the snowplow.

Let's say you're gliding with your skates side by side and about 8 inches apart. Bend your knees.

Then push your skates apart, and slowly turn the toes toward one another. Keep your knees well bent. You should skid to a smooth stop.

If you feel uncertain in executing the snowplow, first get the "feel" of the exercise at the barrier, that it, try it with one hand on the rail.

There's also the one-foot snowplow. Some skaters find it simpler. In this, the toe of only one skate is turned inward. Bend the ankle toward the ice so as to cause the inside edge to bite.

Whether you execute the snowplow with one skate or two, it's strictly for beginners. Later you'll discard it in favor of more sophisticated stopping methods.

SCULLING

Sculling is an exercise that will help you to get the feel of moving forward on the ice.

Put your heels together so that your skates form a 90-degree angle. Drop your ankles slightly so that both your blades are on their inside edges. Bend your knees slightly but keep your body erect. Put your hands out to the side for balance.

Now move both skates forward and out. When your feet are about shoulder-width apart, turn your toes inward and gradually bring your skates parallel. The blades should be flat to the ice as the skates come together.

Push them apart again. Then bring them together.

Continue the in-and-out movement until you can move forward steadily and with confidence.

All skaters fall occasionally, even the very best.

The various instruction books say that you should learn to relax as you fall, which reduces the chance of injury. This is true, of course. But relaxing as you fall is easier said than done. A person has a natural tendency to try to resist falling down, and flails about with his arms in an effort to keep his balance. Relaxing takes experience.

Maybe it will help you to learn to relax—to go limp, actually—if you keep in mind that falls on the ice are not nearly as pain-producing as those that occur on more conventional surfaces. This is

Start sculling from this position.

because the force of the fall is absorbed by the slide you take.

Just as there is a right way to fall, so there is a correct way of getting to your feet. Roll over on one hip, then onto one knee. Bring the opposite skate under you and then, using your hands, push yourself into a standing position.

Move both skates forward and out; then bring them together. Keep repeating the exercise.

STROKING

Stroking, the action which propels you forward along the ice, involves the push, the thrust you make with one blade, and the glide you take with the blade opposite. For the next stroke, the blades change roles.

Begin by standing on the ice, your back straight, your head erect. Keep your knees straight, your legs parallel.

Bending both knees slightly, turn the right foot out so that it forms almost a 90-degree angle with the heel of the left foot.

Push firmly against the ice with the left blade. The inside edge should bite, thrusting you ahead.

As the pushoff ends, instantly transfer your weight to the right blade. Then bring your left foot together with the right; glide.

As your speed begins to slow, repeat the stroke. This time push off with the inside edge of the right blade. Quickly transfer your weight to the left skate; glide.

This stroking cycle is the basis for all the skating you will do, no matter whether it is figure skating, power skating, or speed skating. Practice the stroke as much as you possibly can, always attempting to overcome weak points. The paragraphs that follow cover some of the failings that young skaters sometimes encounter.

Occasionally you may stub a toe pick on the

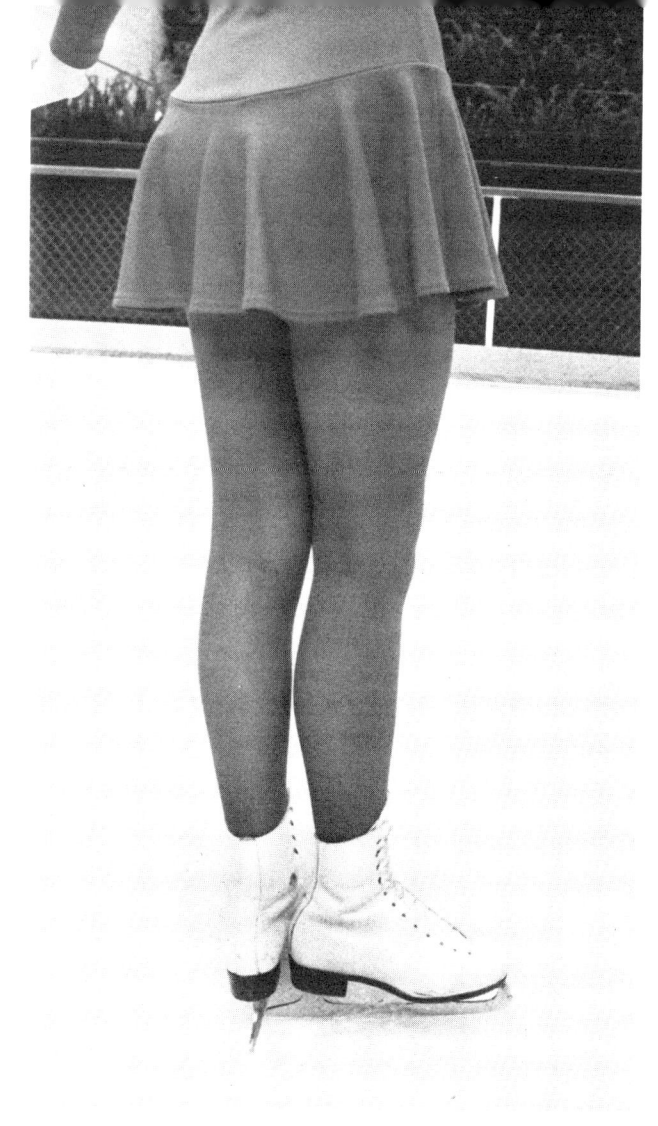

Begin your stroke with your skates in this position.

Push off with the left blade, the inside edge biting, thrusting you forward; glide on the right.

surface of the ice as you're bringing your thrusting foot forward, causing you to stumble and fall. This results from a failure to keep the blade parallel to the ice as it's being returned. Beginners who are unfamiliar with figure skates have a tendency to return the blade toe-down. Instead, you must develop a habit of turning the foot slowly and smoothly, always keeping the blade parallel to the surface.

If you fail to skate in a straight line as you stroke, the problem may be with your hips and shoulders. Always keep them square to the line of travel; that is, never turn your upper body in the direction of the thrusting stroke.

When you keep the shoulders and hips square to the line of travel, you're said to be in a neutral position. If you're working with an instructor, this is a term that you're going to be hearing frequently.

Instructors also use the terms "skating side" and "free side." The skating side is the side of the body above the blade on which you're riding. The free side is the other side, the side above the skate that is off the ice.

The foot on which you're skating is called the skating foot. You'll also hear such terms as skating leg, skating hip, and skating shoulder. On the opposite side, there's the free foot, free leg, free shoulder.

Some beginners become quickly frustrated when they begin stroking because they don't seem to be able to achieve much forward movement, even though they execute torrents of glides and pushoffs in rapid succession. Meanwhile, their friends are whizzing by with long and graceful strides.

The problem here is usually with the pushoff— or lack of it. To get power into your thrusts, you must have your body weight concentrated over the thrusting skate. That's the key factor.

Once you begin skating on your own, always be considerate of other skaters. In public sessions, skaters usually move in a counterclockwise direction at almost all rinks. It's dangerous to try and skate against the general flow when the rink is crowded.

Keep alert to avoid collisions. When you step out onto the ice, hold onto the railing, watching for oncoming skaters. Don't weave in and out among skaters. When you want to stop, move to the side.

Then push off with the right, glide on the left.

Beginners sometimes develop the dangerous habit of looking down at their feet as they skate. You must look straight ahead.

Always skate in control. This means skating at a rate of speed that is appropriate for the rink and the prevailing conditions. In other words, never try to imitate a speed skater at a crowded public session.

When, as a more advanced skater, you're practicing spins, spirals, or other maneuvers, seek out an isolated section of the ice. This may mean one of the rink corners or in the very center. To practice a jump, pick out an empty spot as it is forming. Time your jump so that it's performed in the open area before it fills again.

Don't wear racing blades in a crowded skating session. Their long length and sharp points can cause serious injury should anyone collide with you.

Treat the ice with respect. Sometimes a young skater will, in anger or frustration, dig the toe of a skate into the surface, chipping it. The hazard that results can cause a nasty fall.

Loose items that fall onto the ice also create a hazard. Don't wear pompons, tiny bells, or other such items on your skates, because they frequently fall off. Don't drop any bobby pins. If you wear them while skating, cross them over one another to keep them in place.

T-STOP

Once you've learned to skate smoothly and rhythmically, you should learn a more advanced method of stopping. It's called the T-stop, its name being derived from the T-position in which the blades are placed.

The T-stop is not difficult. As you're gliding forward on your right skate, your knees well bent, ease your left skate behind the right and turn the toe to the left. Now lower the blade to the ice, and when it touches, draw it toward the front skate.

The first few times that you try the T-stop, put the flat of the blade to the ice. Once you've become skilled in the exercise, adjust the blade so that it's the outside edge that makes contact. You'll get more bite and a quicker stop, so be prepared for it.

A key factor in executing the T-stop is the ability to gradually change your weight to the rear foot. The more weight you concentrate there, the quicker you'll stop. Advanced skaters are able to lean back to such a degree that they can lift the front foot from the ice. Naturally, they stop abruptly.

When executing the T-stop, it's the outside edge of the rear skate that brakes your forward motion.

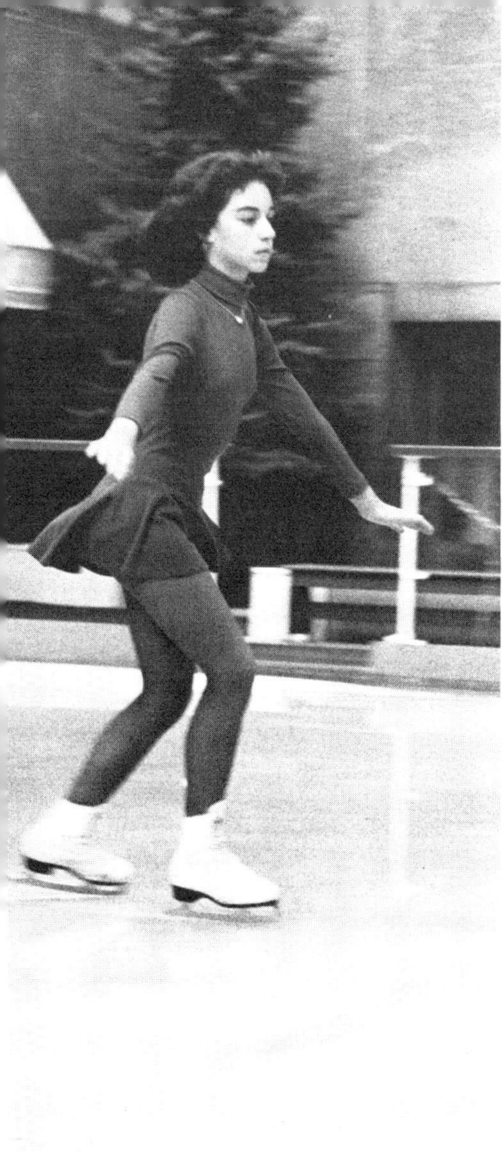

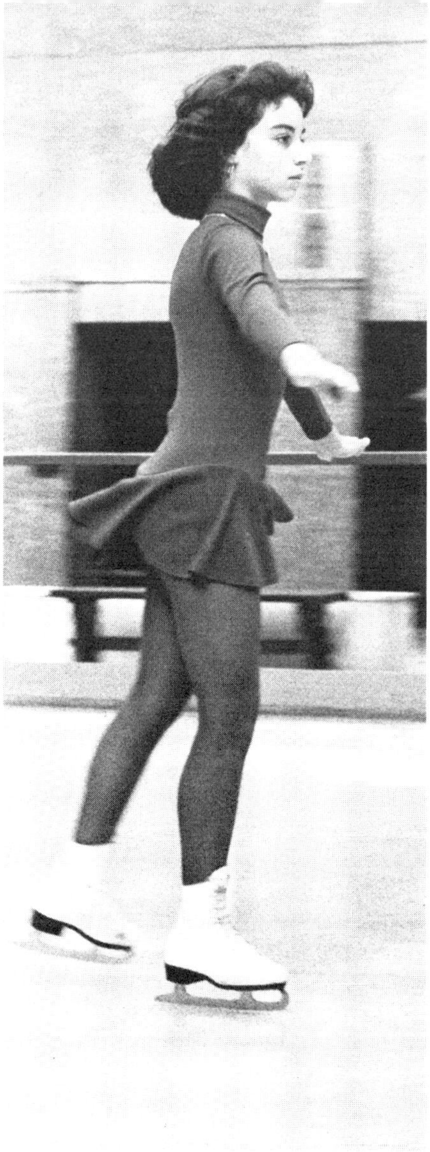

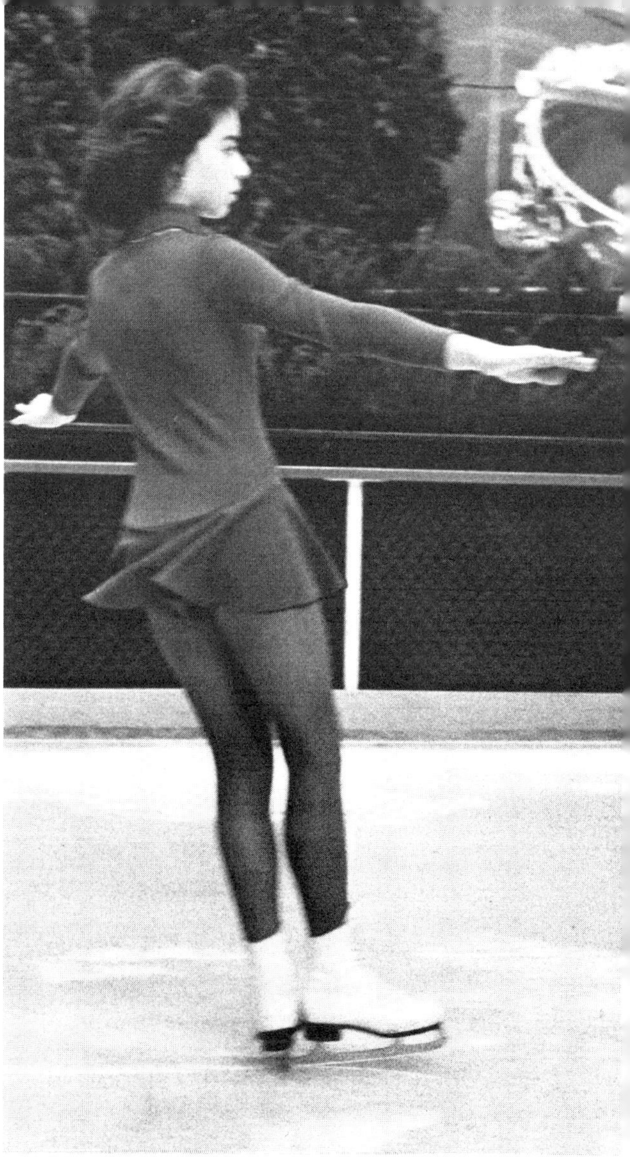

HOCKEY STOP

The hockey stop is an efficient way to stop and a dramatic one as well, ending in a spray of flying ice. While it's the usual method of stopping in the game of hockey, it's also common to figure skating. No matter how fast you're moving, the hockey stop will brake you down in short order.

As you glide along, bring your skates side by side, then abruptly turn both heels sharply to the right; bend your knees. Keep your knees bent until you have stopped completely. You can also execute the hockey stop in the other direction, if it feels more comfortable and is easier.

While it is an easy maneuver to describe and, indeed, does not demand great skill, the hockey stop is sometimes difficult for beginners. What it does require is confidence. If you fail to turn your blades the full 90 degrees, or fail to do it abruptly, you'll end up merely turning, not stopping.

Before attempting a hockey stop from a glide, practice from a standing-still position. Stand with the skates parallel, and then quickly turn the blades to the right or left. Turn them a full 90 degrees. Once you get the "feel" of how the skates turn, try the maneuver from a glide.

You can execute the hockey stop by turning either right or left. But you must turn quickly and abruptly.

When sculling backward, start with your toes together, your heels apart. Thrust your skates apart, then draw them together again.

SKATING BACKWARD

As soon as you've learned how to glide forward and stop, you should learn to skate backward.

Some young skaters are hesitant about learning to skate in a reverse direction. They feel awkward; they feel unsure of themselves.

You can help to overcome any misgivings you might have by first learning to scull backward. Start with your toes together, your heels well apart, and both blades on the inside edges. It's rather a knock-kneed position.

Move your skates apart, pressing the inside edges of the blades into the ice. As your skates are thrust apart, you'll begin moving backward.

When your skates are about shoulder-width apart, straighten your knees, shift to the flats of your blades, and draw your skates together again. Then, without pausing, repeat the exercise, bending your knees and thrusting outward. You should soon be

In skating backward, begin by gliding. Push off with one blade (the right blade as shown above), and then return it to its original position alongside the other. Then push off with the other blade.

able to scull efficiently from one end of the rink to the other.

To execute a backward skating stroke, begin by gliding backward, your skates side by side, a few inches apart. Your shoulders should be square to your line of travel.

Bend the knees slightly and concentrate your weight over one skate. Push off with that skate. As you glide backward, return the skate to its original position alongside the other.

Now push off with the other skate and return *it* to its original position. With practice you'll learn to alternate strokes, building speed and maintaining it.

In executing the toe scratch with one foot, first slide the free skate behind you. Lean forward; lift the heel of the skating foot, allowing the toe picks to scrape the ice.

BACKWARD STOPPING

When skating backward, the toe scratch is the easiest and most efficient method of stopping. You can execute the toe scratch with either one skate or both.

In doing it with one skate, first slide the free blade behind you as you're gliding. Lean forward slightly and lift the heel of the skating foot, allowing the toe picks to scrape the ice. This will slow and ultimately brake your forward movement.

Don't try this method of stopping while gliding with the skates side by side. It's vital that you slide one skate behind the other first; otherwise, you're likely to topple forward.

In doing the toe scratch with both skates, glide backward with the skates side by side. Lean forward; tilt your heels off the ice so that your weight becomes concentrated on your toe picks.

You may find it easier to do the toe scratch on both blades. This time begin by gliding with the skates side by side, only a few inches apart. Your body should be perfectly straight, your arms outstretched.

As you begin to slow down, maintain the straight-line position of your body, and lift your heels. As your weight becomes concentrated on the toe picks, you'll slow to a stop.

The first time you try these stops, keep your speed down. As your efficiency increases, increase your speed.

SKATING EDGES

By this time, you're sure to realize that the term "edge" has more than one meaning.

First, it's a technical term that refers to either one of the opposing sharp sides of the hollow-ground skate blade, to the two cutting edges of the blade, that is.

The term is also used in describing the curve that results when the skater leans in one direction or the other so as to cause a particular blade edge to cut into the ice. In this sense, edge means curve.

The four basic edges, each named for the particular edge being used and the direction in which the skater is traveling, are as follows:

>   forward outside edge
>   forward inside edge
>   back outside edge
>   back inside edge

Either of these edges can be skated on either the right or left blades. Thus, a curve will be described as a right forward inside edge, or a left back outside edge, and so on.

Practice skating with an exercise known as "scootering." Simply push off with one blade and glide on the other, maintaining the edge you wish to skate. Scootering helps you to get the "feel" of an edge.

FORWARD OUTSIDE EDGE—Of the four basic edges, the one skated on the forward outside edge is the most important. It emphasizes a sideways body lean, a position that is fundamental to many advanced maneuvers.

Try it on your right foot first. Get up speed with a series of strong strokes. Then, gliding with the skates side by side, curve gently to the right. In other words, your right hip, shoulder, and arm will be in front; press your left shoulder back. Turn your head so that you are looking over your right shoulder toward the center of the circle you are about to skate.

Strike off on the right outside edge by leaning to the right, that is, toward the center of the circle. Allow the left foot and leg to take a position behind, the left toe positioned above the tracing being cut by the right skate. The left heel should be just inside the tracing.

Carry your right hand out in front of your body. Press your left hip back.

Beginners often find it difficult to hold this position for a sustained period. As you begin skating on the edge, there's a tendency for the hips and shoulders to swing around in the direction of the curve. As a result, you veer off toward the center of the circle that you're attempting to skate.

This tendency is known as "swing," and you have to consciously work to resist it. The trouble almost always begins with the free hip. You have your free leg positioned behind you properly, but the free hip, without you even realizing it, begins to roll

The forward outside edge, skated on the right blade, is the first edge to learn.

forward, and once that happens the free shoulder and arm are going to follow. What you have to do is lock the free hip into position as soon as you begin skating on the edge, and then determinedly keep its forward movement checked.

When teaching this and other edges, instructors urge their pupils to "lean in one piece." This means to lean with the entire body. In performing outside edges, some beginners drop their skating hip, which causes them to lean into the circle, but only from the waist down. From above the waist, they're leaning in the opposite direction, out of the circle. This failing can also apply to backward outside edges.

The first few times you attempt to execute the forward outside edge, the circle you trace is likely to be a very big one, its diameter from 20 to 25 feet. Try to reduce the circle to 15 feet, or thereabouts. One rule of thumb says that the diameter of the circle should be about three times your height.

FORWARD INSIDE EDGE—This is the easiest of all the edges. Try it on the right skate while curving to the left.

Build up your speed and then glide with your skates side by side. Keep your shoulders square to your line of travel and lean toward the inside of the circle.

Strike out on the inside edge of your right foot, and carry your free leg with the knee slightly bent so that the free foot is over the tracing.

Again, watch out for any tendency to swing.

The left back outside edge begins from a series of back crossovers; notice the body's lean.

Strive to keep your hips square to the direction in which you're moving. Don't permit the free foot to move forward. If it starts to move, you're in trouble.

Once you're moving on the edge, turn your head so you're looking toward the center of the circle, which will enable you to see where you're going. But it's only your head you turn, not your shoulders.

BACK OUTSIDE EDGE—Try this edge on the right skate while moving in a counterclockwise direction.

Build up speed with a series of crossover strokes (which are explained in the next chapter), and then glide on the outside edge of the right skate. While your hips should be kept square to the tracing, you must turn your head and shoulders toward the direction in which you're moving. Lean into the center of the circle.

The chief problem that most skaters encounter with this exercise is in having the hips follow the upper body's turn. To overcome this tendency, you must maintain the utmost forward pressure on the free hip.

BACK INSIDE EDGE—Beginners often find this the most difficult edge of all. The back inside should first be attempted on the right skate while moving in a clockwise direction.

Build your speed with a series of crossover strokes. Then glide and lean toward the center of the circle. As you strike off on the inside edge of the right skate, extend your free leg in back of your body. Straighten the knee. Your free arm and shoulder turn, too. Look over your free shoulder to see where you're headed. Keep plenty of pressure on your free hip.

These are the four basic edges. Once you've mastered them with your right skate, switch to the left. You should become equally adept with both.

CROSSOVERS

By skating crossovers, you're able to round the corners at the rink ends and also skate complete circles.

A crossover is just what the name implies: the crossing of one foot—the free foot—around and in front of the other. When you execute a series of crossovers in rapid succession, it's something like walking up a flight of stairs sideways.

Almost all skaters find that it's easier to do crossovers to the left, in a counterclockwise direction, that is. But you should seek to become skilled in both directions.

When executing a forward crossover to the left, as described below, your right shoulder and arm will be in a lead position throughout.

Begin by gliding with the skates side by side, then lean toward the center of the circle that you are about to skate. Push off on the outside edge of your left blade.

As your weight becomes centered over your left

In skating a forward crossover in a counterclockwise direction, you keep crossing the free right foot in front of the left.

The back crossover stroke in a clockwise direction. Be sure to lean toward the center of the circle.

skate, cross the free right foot in front of the left. Then simply bring the skates together and get ready to repeat the stroke.

As you keep repeating the action, the curve you're skating becomes a circle. Always lean toward the center of the circle as you skate, maintaining the same amount of lean through every phase of each of your strokes. Leaning will help to make your moves crisp and decisive.

You'll also help yourself if you'll remember to

always bend the knee of the forward leg. Bend it deeply. If you fail to bend the knee, you can get on the wrong edge.

Once you can skate crossovers in a counterclockwise direction, reverse the sequence and do them to the right. This time your left arm and shoulder lead. Push off on the outside edge of the right blade; pick up your free left foot, cross it over the right, and skate on the inside edge. The right foot, now behind, is then picked up and placed in front again on its outside edge. Don't forget to lean toward the center.

BACK CROSSOVERS—Try back crossovers in a clockwise direction first. Your right arm and shoulder lead. Be sure to lean toward the center of the circle.

As you skate backward, lift your right foot and cross it in back of your left, placing it down to the inside of the curve. Keep repeating the action.

THE THREE-TURN

The three-turn dates to a period when it was fashionable to trace numbers on the ice in displaying one's figure skating skills. What you do when executing a three-turn is change your direction from forward to backward, or vice versa, while remaining on the same foot. As this may suggest, the three-turn is one of skating's most graceful maneuvers.

A figure 3 tracing like this should be etched upon the ice when executing a three-turn.

A three-turn can begin on any edge, but the most commonly used three is diagrammed here. It starts on the right forward outside edge (RFO) and finishes on the right back inside edge (RBI).

To execute this turn, take several forward strokes in a clockwise direction, then glide on the outside edge of your right blade. Your left foot trails behind. Lean toward the center of the circle being skated.

Turn your left hip toward the center of the circle,

and look in that direction.

Bring your free foot (your left foot) into a T-position behind your skating foot. Now turn your right blade a full 90 degrees to the left. Quickly spin your shoulders in the opposite direction, to the right. This causes you to glide backward on your right inside edge.

Beginners frequently fail to turn their shoulders properly when seeking to execute a three-turn. When you turn your shoulders toward the center of the circle you're skating, you're storing the power that will trigger the turn. When you turn the shoulders back, you're unleashing that power. You have to turn decisively in both directions.

This is a three-turn in a clockwise direction from the right forward outside edge. The shoulders lead the turn, which ends on the right back inside.

TWO-FOOT SPIN

The swift whirling motion that characterizes a spin is not difficult to learn. But what can be a problem is the dizziness that can accompany fast spinning.

To help prevent the dizziness, always keep your eyes open and allow your head to revolve at the same rate of speed as your body. What you shouldn't do is spin the way a ballet performer does, his body turning first, then his head snapping around.

To be able to spin with the ease of show skaters in the Ice Capades, you must use the flat of your blades, not the edges. The simplest spin is the two-foot spin. Stand with your feet side by side and about shoulder width apart. Extend your hands out in front of your body, keeping them about chest level, the fingers not quite touching, the palms down. Start to swing your arms from side to side. When your arms swing to the left, allow your weight to shift to the left. When your arms go right, shift your weight right.

Build up momentum with each swing. On the third or fourth swing, bring your feet close together and allow the energy generated by your arms to start you spinning. Be sure you're on the flats of your blades.

On your first attempt, you may only spin a half revolution or so. But with practice you'll quickly improve.

It will help you if you remember to stand perfectly straight, your head and shoulders directly over your skates. Also keep your skates the same distance apart throughout the spin, but let them turn separately, instead of attempting to keep them side by side.

You'll notice that advanced skaters bring their arms to their bodies as they spin. But, as a beginner, you'll find that your spins are smoother and longer if you keep your arms extended.

By swinging your arms first to the right and then to the left, you build up the momentum that powers your spin. Keep your arms outstretched as you revolve. And keep your eyes open.

41

This is how you should finish the spin.

After you've become skilled in spinning with two feet, able to revolve eight or nine times on each attempt, try the one-foot spin. You can launch into a one-foot spin by first spinning on two feet, and then simply lifting one skate and holding that foot against the other knee as you revolve.

The more sophisticated method is to begin with a three-turn and a few back crossovers, all done to the left. On the third back crossover, done on the right foot, held the inside edge. Bring the free leg forward and step inside the circle you're making with the crossovers, turning to your left to begin a revolution. Your free arm leads the way.

Once you begin the spin, swing the new free leg (the right leg), with the knee bent, in the direction you're turning. This helps to increase your speed. Then bend the knee in front of the other leg, positioning the right skate at about the left knee.

BUNNY HOP

Jumps in skating are what the home run is to baseball—a concentrated burst of skill from the performer, and a moment of high excitement for the spectator. As with all skating maneuvers, jumps have to be performed with grace and even elegance, with takeoffs and landings executed cleanly and effortlessly.

There are more than 25 jumps common to figure skating. Some of them, such as the axel and salchow, are named for their originators (Axel Paulsen and Ulrich Salchow).

The bunny hop is a jump that beginners can do.

<------------- • R -------------<------------- L

When you begin the bunny hop on your left blade (L), touch down momentarily on the toe picks of your right skate (R), then continue on the left.

Executed from the flat of the blade (not an edge), it's one of the few jumps that does not require the

To trigger the bunny hop, throw the free leg forward. Land on the toe pick of that foot, then push—"hop"—to the flat of the starting blade.

skater to turn in the air. What you do is leap forward on one foot, landing on the blade of that foot. The toe pick of the other skate assists in the jump.

Begin from a T-position, the left foot in front, the right foot back. Push off with the right blade, bending the left knee. Throw the free leg—the right leg forward—and jump from the left knee.

Land on the flat of the left blade, but touch down briefly on the toe picks of the right skate. As you may realize, your position at the start and finish of the jump are exactly the same.

To keep maximum control of your body during the jump, remember to keep your upper body erect. Don't bend forward from the waist; don't look down.

FORWARD SPIRAL

The spiral is a graceful position in which you execute a series of unbroken circular glides. Your free foot is extended behind your body, the leg straight, the foot itself positioned at almost head level.

The arms are extended out from the body, the hands held at about shoulder level. The head and shoulders are erect.

As you glide, keep pressure on your skating heel; otherwise, you can lose your balance.

If you're knowledgeable about ballet, you'll recognize the spiral position as being similar to the arabesque. It stresses control and balance, and helps on the way for the execution of advanced turns and jumps and other sophisticated maneuvers.

The forward spiral: keep your head and shoulders erect, your back arched.

WALTZ JUMP

The waltz jump is an advanced jump in which you take off from a forward outside edge, execute a half turn in the air, then land on the back outside edge of the other foot.

When you're performing the waltz jump in a counterclockwise direction, first skate on the right forward outside edge, then step onto the left forward outside. Next, swing your free leg—your right leg—

forward, and push off with the left. Make a half turn in the air, and land on the right back outside.

The waltz jump is important because you land on the back outside, one of the chief characteristics of many advanced jumps.

In the waltz jump, swinging the free leg forward helps to provide the momentum for the jump itself and the in-the-air half turn. Landing on the back outside edge is a characteristic of many advanced jumps.

PIVOTS

When you execute a pivot, your action is similar to the movement of the A-shaped compass you probably use for drawing circles in mathematics class. You dig the toe picks of one skate firmly in the ice, then circle that skate, powering your revolutions with the other blade.

Try a forward inside pivot first. With your skates side by side and about shoulder width apart, place your right toe picks in the ice, then turn the left skate so the blade faces the right (something like a T-position). Bend the right knee and concentrate your weight on the right toe.

As you push off with your left skate, swing your left arm and left shoulder forward, and your right arm and shoulder back. But be sure to keep the shoulders level.

If you fail to move smoothly, or if your left skate tends to veer to the left, it may be because you're not putting sufficient weight on the right toe. It's a "must" that your weight be concentrated there. And you must also keep the right knee deeply bent.

You can also perform a pivot in a reverse direction, in which case it's called a back inside pivot.

In the pivot, you place the toe picks of one skate in the ice, then circle around it.

THE FIGURE 8

Figure skating used to be exactly that. People actually skated intricate figures, just as if they were drawing them on the ice with their skates. These included not only numerical figures, but lacy designs like four-leaf clovers and grapevines.

Figure skating is much different today. There are two types: compulsory figures (also called school figures) and free style (or free skating). Compulsory figures, standardized by national and international organizations, take the form of circles and half circles and their variations that are skated in assorted combinations, each with rulebook precision.

All of the compulsory figures are based upon the figure 8, which consists of two adjoining circles of equal size. The figure 8 has two axes, a long axis and a short axis. The long axis is an imaginary line which, if drawn through the center of the two circles, would bisect them evenly. The short axis, a second imaginary line, runs perpendicular to the long axis at the midpoint of the figure. In skating a figure 8, you must maintain these axes as described here; otherwise, your circles won't be of equal size or in the right place.

The long axis of each circle (which, of course, is equal to the diameter) should be about three times the skater's height. Tall skaters are permitted to skate smaller circles.

In performing an 8, the skater pushes off from the point where the two circles intersect, and glides through the first circle on the right skate. At the intersecting point, the left skate is put to the ice and the skater pushes off on the right, gliding through the second circle.

There are four ways in which the circle 8 can be skated: (1) RFO-LFO (from a right forward outside edge to a left forward outside edge); (2) RFI-LFI; (3) RBO-LBO; and (4) RBI-LBI. Both the RFO-LFO and RFI-LFI figure 8s are included in the USFSA's Preliminary Test.

In skating an 8, first stand at the point where the long and short axes intersect, and survey the ice in both directions, drawing a picture of each circle in your mind's eye.

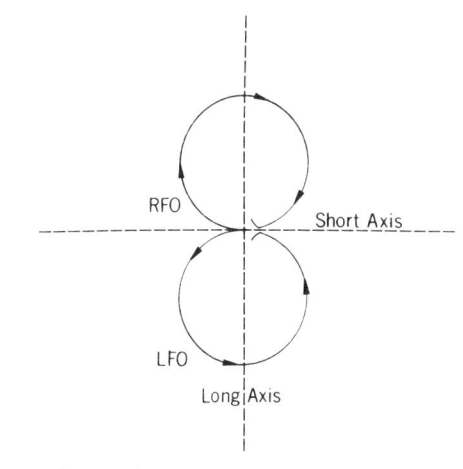

A figure 8

To skate the RFO-LFO figure 8, stand with your skates in a T-position, and push off from the left blade and glide on the right; glide through the entire circle. Lean into the circle; carry your left leg behind your body. (Reading again the section in this book titled "Skating Edges" may be helpful to you.)

When you approach the point where the two circles meet, swing the left leg forward. Reverse the position of your arms and shoulders so that the left shoulder leads. As you cross the point, put your left skate alongside your right and push off with the right blade, gliding on the outside edge of the left. The right foot now trails.

When performing a figure 8 in competition, the figure must be skated three times. If, on your first attempt, one or both of the circles is poorly skated, don't retrace it. Instead, correct whatever errors you've made.

One frequent mistake is the tendency to close a circle too soon, making it have a 6 shape instead of being perfectly round. You can help to overcome this if you keep in mind where the short axis is located, and remember to skate along it for a brief instant at the point where the circles meet.

Another error is the failure to keep the two circles properly aligned. In other words, if the long axis were actually traced upon the ice, it would bend to either the right or left.

A figure 8 on the right forward outside. You glide through the entire circle.

COMPETITIVE FIGURE SKATING

Of course, the figure 8 is merely the beginning. Advanced figures involve circles with tricky edge changes, quick three-turns, and graceful loops. And there's much more. There's also free skating, or free-style competition, in which each skater develops his own program of jumps, spins, spirals, or dances, all of which are performed to music of his own choosing. The free-style presentation, which lasts about five minutes, counts for 50 percent of the point total by which competitors are judged.

You can be as varied and as imaginative as you want in developing your program. But since skaters are judged on the cleanness and sureness of execution, it makes no sense in attempting moves that are beyond one's capability.

Besides the technical merit of one's presentations, skaters are also judged on composition and style. Does one particular movement lead naturally to the next? Does one's presentation reflect the character and style of the music? The skater has to move easily and rhythmically throughout, the body always graceful and controlled.

One other aspect of figure skating must be mentioned—ice dancing. Ice dancing is figure skating with a partner, and can consist of spins and jumps, pivots and spirals. In competition, there are compulsory figures and free style dancing, with couples judged on the basis of rhythm, execution, composition, and style.

Championship competition; a free-style performance.

Ice dancing

Pair skating

Pair skating involves working with a partner, too, and often the term is used as a synonym for ice dancing. The U.S. Figure Skating Association defines pair skating as "a branch of figure skating executed simultaneously and in harmony by two skaters that involves various lifts, spins, and free-style movements."

Pair skating is sometimes referred to as shadow skating when the two partners maintain identical positions and perform the same movements. It's known as mirror skating when the partners' positions are the reverse of one another.

Skating competition begins on a local level, then advances in stages through sectional and regional championships to the U.S. Nationals. Competitors are of all ages. The only requirements are that you have the skill necessary to qualify for competition, and that you be a member of the USFSA or a member of a club or skating team approved by the organization.

The USFSA's official test schedule is made up of a total of 70 figures. Some are easy to execute; others seem unreal in their complexity.

The 70 figures are divided into a series of nine tests, beginning with the Preliminary Test and then ranging from the First through the Eighth (or Gold). Some of the tests also call for free skating demonstrations. An award is given for passing each test.

A skater requires a good deal of training and experience to be able to pass even the Preliminary Test. In recognition of this fact, the U.S. Figure Skating Association recently began making available a second series of tests which examine skaters' skills beginning at very modest levels. For example, you can pass the first Beginner's Test by demonstrating the ability to skate forward and stop successfully.

These tests are not only for members of the USFSA, but for the general public as well. Not only do you gain a certain satisfaction out of passing one of these tests, but you also receive an attractive badge. For more information on the test program, inquire at your local rink, or you can write the USFSA (Sears Crescent, Suite 500, City Hall Plaza, Boston, Massachusetts 02108), requesting descriptive material on what's called the "Basic Test Program."

If you plan to enter skating competition, you should be aware of the method of scoring, which is similar to that used in diving. A panel of judges awards points for each skater's performance. The points are multiplied by a degree of difficulty factor in figuring the skater's performance rating.

The degree of difficulty factor is expressed in a numerical scale ranging from 1 to 6. The simplest figures have a factor of 1; the most difficult figures, a factor of 6.

Each skater's technical skill and personal style is likewise evaluated numerically. This scale is used:

> 0—figure not skated
> 1—bad performance
> 2—poor performance
> 3—average performance
> 4—good performance
> 5—very good performance
> 6—perfect performance

Suppose a judge thinks you have performed a figure having a degree of difficulty factor of 2, in somewhere between a "very good" and "perfect" manner. You might receive a score of 5.1 or 5.2. The idea, of course, is to earn higher marks than any of the other competitors.

What do judges look for as a figure is being done? Many things. Did the skater start correctly, beginning from a standstill with a single stroke from the blade edge? Is the skater's body position correct, the head up, back straight, arms in a natural position, palms down?

The figure has to be skated three times on each foot without any pauses. Afterward the judges check that skater's tracings. They want to find out whether all the circles are the same size and shape, with each point of each circle tracing equidistant from the circle's center. The tracing will also reveal whether the skater maintained a true edge throughout, or was guilty of skating on the flats or wobbling.

As all of this may imply, you have to be talented in order to succeed as a figure skater, with success implying the winning of a national championship. But talent isn't the only requirement.

It also takes the determination necessary to undergo the rugged training grind. It's usual for a boy or girl with championship potential to train at least six hours a day, seven days a week. The program is likely to include two lessons a day, special summer skating camps, and perhaps a private school. Superstar Janet Lynn, who won several national amateur championships, began taking private lessons at the age of four and at twelve was national junior champion.

Then there is the financial hurdle. It can cost as much as $10,000 a year to school a young skater for championship competition. By the time he or she has become a teen-ager and is competing in the U.S. Nationals, the training program may have cost as much as $100,000.

POWER SKATING

"Some young skaters believe that success in hockey depends on one's ability to shoot, pass, or stickhandle," says Emile Francis, the former general manager of the New York Rangers. "These are important, of course, but skating is what's vital."

Other experts agree. Some say that skating is as much as 75 percent of the game.

Skating in hockey means power skating. It means skating with speed and strength.

To be able to skate with power, you must put plenty of thrust into each push. This mean thrusting from the entire blade and straightening the leg as the thrust is ending.

Begin by facing forward and putting the heels of your skates together so that an angle of about 90 degrees is formed.

Bend your knees slightly, but keep your back straight, your head erect. Bend the ankle of the pushing foot toward the ice.

When you push off, push from the entire blade, with the thrust beginning at the back of the blade and ending at the toe. When you push in this manner, you're assuring that the big thigh muscles will be involved, not merely the smaller muscles of the lower leg.

Continue pushing until the leg straightens. By this

Push off from the entire blade; straighten the leg.

time, you will have shifted your weight so that it is concentrated over the other skate, and you'll be gliding. The longer the pushing leg remains extended, the longer you'll glide.

When you want to end the glide, simply bring the pushing foot alongside the gliding foot. Bend the knees and push off into the next stride.

You can further increase the efficiency of your strides by moving your arms and shoulders in rhythm with your legs. When you push off with the right leg, move your left arm forward. When you push with the left leg, the right arm goes forward.

Use your arms and shoulders to help increase your momentum.

While this arm action can be important toward attaining power and speed, don't overdo it. Excessive motion with your arms will hinder your ability to stickhandle.

Also avoid tilting your shoulders when you move your arms. Keep them parallel to the ice; otherwise, your balance will be adversely affected.

Also bend forward as you skate. Figure skaters, because their skates have toe picks which can cause them to stumble, aren't able to utilize a forward lean. But hockey players can.

SKATING BACKWARD—All hockey players have to know how to sail over the ice while skating backward. It's a vital skill for defensemen, of course, but forwards have to have this ability, too. It frequently happens that a forward can prevent an opponent from shooting through his ability to skate backward.

If you feel unsure of yourself when traveling backward, try sculling backward first. (See the section earlier in the book titled "Sculling.")

When skating backward, the position of your body should be similar to the one you would take when sitting in a straight-back chair. However, you must remember to lean slightly forward. Always keep your head up. Your stick blade should be on the ice.

Bend the left knee; push off from the inside edge of the left blade. Glide. Push off from the inside edge of the other blade, the right blade; glide.

To be able to move fast while skating backward,

you must develop plenty of hip action, throwing the hips from one side to the other as you push off and glide. Getting your hips involved helps to assure smooth strokes and long glides.

TURNING—When you want to turn to either the right or left, use the turning technique described earlier in this book in the section titled "Crossovers." When using crossovers, you can turn without having to reduce speed.

Suppose you want to turn to the right. Concentrate your weight on your right foot and bend your right knee. Then, leaning in the direction of the turn, bring the left foot forward and cross it in front of the right, putting the inside edge to the ice and pushing off in the direction of the turn.

The faster you're moving when you start the turn, the more you must flex the inside knee, the right knee in the example above. And the more weight you must put on the inside foot.

What about stopping? What's called the "hockey stop" is described earlier in this book. As you're whisking down the ice, you draw your skates together, then suddenly snap the blades sideways, digging the edges into the ice at right angles to the course you're traveling. You have to bend your knees and lean back in order to keep your balance.

A forward crossover

A back crossover

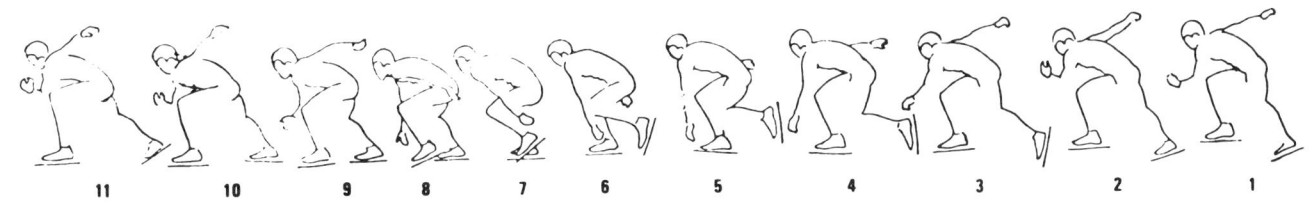

In speed skating, the body is bent at the waist, the knees kept forward. Entire blade is used in pushing off. Weight shift must be smooth and rhythmic.

SPEED SKATING

Speed skating is a sport for all ages, with separate events for boys and girls, and men and women. Previous experience as a speed skater is not necessary but, naturally, some ability in skating itself is important in getting started.

"The willingness to practice and an enthusiasm for the sport count for a great deal," says an official of the Canadian Amateur Speed Skating Association. "It's not uncommon for a diligent skater to win medals and even trophies in his or her second or third year."

Competition is often organized into these age groups:

Senior	18 and over
Intermediate	16–17 years
Junior	14–15 years
Juvenile	12–13 years
Midget	10–11 years
Bantam	8–9 years
Peewee	7 and under

Through the years, several different types of speed skating have evolved. The most important today are the outdoor mass start, the indoor mass start, and the Olympic-style event.

The outdoor mass start is held on an outdoor oval course which measures in distance from 250 to 400 meters. Contestants all start at the same time and the first to cross the finish line wins. There are no individual lanes for skaters. The indoor mass start is the same, but with competition adapted to a shorter indoor course.

Contestants in Olympic-style events race the clock over a measured course. While there can be any number of entrants, only two skaters are on the course at the same time, each skating in his own lane. It can be either an oval course or a straightaway. The contestant with the best recorded time wins.

The proper body position for speed skating calls for keeping the knees well forward and bending deeply at the waist. The head is kept lifted slightly.

Push off with the entire blade. Keep pushing the leg until it's almost straight.

When placing the free skate on the ice, don't put it down too far ahead of the other skate. It should be placed down almost alongside the other. Keep the foot and leg relaxed as you bring it forward.

The transfer of your body weight from one skate to the other must be done smoothly and rhythmically. Beginners have to be careful not to bob up and down. The head should be kept perfectly level as you race along, with all of the power you're generating going toward moving you forward.

Long-bladed skates assure the utmost speed.

In sprint events, explosive start is vital.

Getting a good glide is vital. Be sure to keep low to the ice, but don't lean forward. Your weight has to be kept concentrated over your skates in order to glide efficiently.

In sprint races, the start is critical. On the command of "On your mark!," skate up to the starting line. Position your skates so that the blades form an angle of about 45 degrees with the line. The toe of your left skate should be just behind the line. Press the inside edges of your blades into the ice.

Bend your knees slightly and bend forward a bit from the waist. Lift your arms, keeping the right arm slightly higher than the left.

At the command of "Ready," fix your gaze at a point about 15 yards beyond the starting line. Overall, your body should be like a compressed spring, ready to release.

At the instant the starter's gun fires, explode away. Push off with the right skate, straightening your body slightly, and swing the left foot past the starting line.

Don't glide on the left blade. Instead, push off on the inside edge almost as soon as the blade is placed on the ice. The first three or four strides should be short, hard-driving strides, meant to build your speed as quickly as possible. Keeping the blades low to the ice as you bring each one forward will help to make for fast strides. Swing your arms vigorously to add momentum.

Gradually increase the length of your glides. In-

Young speedsters compete in an indoor sprint event.

crease the length of each arm's swing, too. On the backswing, the arm should go back as far as possible. On the forward swing, the hand should cross in front of the knee opposite.

In skating distance events, alter your style somewhat. Your strategy in sprint races must be to travel at maximum speed from beginning to end, but in any event from 1,000 to 10,000 meters, the idea is to establish a comfortable pace and maintain it throughout.

The start doesn't have to be quite as frantic as in a sprint. You can glide longer on each stride.

In skating a turn, your speed should be exactly the same as it is on the straightaways. Lean well to

Skaters lean to the inside in negotiating a turn.

the inside and turn by crossing the free foot in front of the skating foot (a technique covered in this book in the section titled "Crossovers").

After completing the first turn, cross your hands over the small of your back. Keep them in that position throughout the race. This helps to keep your stride smooth and rhythmic.

Speed skating is about as strenuous as any other sport you can name. It takes a year-round conditioning program to be able to compete on a championship level, a program that stresses daily running and calisthenics to build stamina.

Speed skating record holders rank as the fastest self-propelled humans over level terrain. In short races, they average speeds of very close to 30 miles per hour. A racer will complete a mile event in about one minute less than the track runner.

American speed skaters can perform with brilliance in international competition. Over the years the United States has taken more medals in speed skating than in any other event in the Winter Olympics. In 1976 Sheila Young of the United States won three Olympic medals, gold, silver, and bronze.

For additional information about speed skating in the United States, write the Amateur Skating Union of the United States (4432 West Deming Place, Chicago, Illinois 60639).

Competitive speed skating in Canada is supervised by the Canadian Amateur Speed Skating Association (46 Graystone Gardens, Toronto, Ontario M8Z 3C4).

Rhythmic striding is obvious here.

SOME HISTORY

Skating used to be a sport that was limited to those parts of the country that had cold winters with freezing temperatures. Minnesota, Wisconsin, Michigan, New York, and the New England states were where almost all of the country's skaters were to be found.

Modern rinks, with their artificially frozen ice, changed all this. The first ice rink was installed in the old Madison Square Garden in New York City in 1879. Today, there are hundreds of such rinks in operation, permitting skating everywhere at any time, no matter what the outside temperature happens to be.

While this development and others important to the sport's growth and popularity are of fairly recent vintage, skating's evolution has covered many centuries.

Skating is one of the several sports to have been developed out of an early method of transportation. (Running, swimming, skiing, and horse racing are some others.) For hundreds of years, the people of Scandinavian countries crossed frozen lakes, rivers, and canals by using polished animal shankbones which they strapped to their feet. Archeologists have discovered such specimens, shaped very much like modern skates, in both northwestern and central Europe. They date to before the birth of Christ.

Because bone skates did not cut into the ice and grip it properly, the skater could not glide. Instead, he pushed himself along using a stout staff.

The Dutch advanced skate technology by constructing them of wood. Skates with iron blades were also first manufactured by the Dutch.

Scotland was where skating as a sport originated. The Skating Club of Edinburgh, formed in 1642, was the first such organization of its type. Before the century ended, many similar clubs were operating throughout northern Europe.

Ice skating in Canada is said to date to 1604 when Sieur de Monte, a French explorer, settled on St. Croix Island. As a means of transportation, he and his men copied the Iroquois who used bone skates for hunting deer in the winter. Skating did not begin to become regarded as a recreational activity in Canada until late in the seventeenth century when British soldiers stationed there were observed enjoying skating in their leisure time.

The introduction of the covered rink, which gave some protection against the severe winter cold, did much to help make skating popular in Canada. The first covered rink was built in Quebec City, Quebec, in 1858. Some of the covered rinks were heated and lighted for night skating. Great numbers of women began to skate for the first time.

Up until the middle of the nineteenth century, all skates had the same failing: They either slipped off the foot or had to be strapped so tightly that the toes became numb. The first all-metal skates with

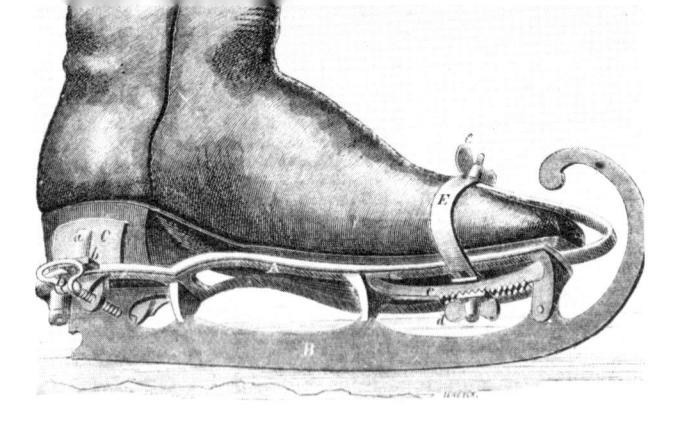

A clamp-on skate of the 1850s.

blades of steel helped to overcome this problem. Developed by E. W. Bushnell in Philadelphia in 1848, these skates eliminated the wooden footplate and, in time, led to the invention of skates that could be fastened to the shoe or boot by clamps.

Although Bushnell charged $30 a pair for his skates, a large amount of money at the time, he received more orders than he could fill. Other manufacturers began making steel skates, and within the next decade or two they were being sold everywhere in the world that there was ice.

Improvements in skates led to improvements in skating techniques. Now skaters could twist and turn as never before.

An American ballet master named Jackson Haines helped to revolutionize skating. He realized that skating could be done to music, that the waltz, for instance, could be performed on ice, as could other dance movements. When Haines instructed his pupils, he instructed them to glide, twist, and spiral as ballet dancers did. He gave skating exhibitions along the East Coast of the United States and in Canada and then in 1864, when the Civil War was in progress, he toured Europe, introducing his theories to huge crowds, who acclaimed him wildly.

Haines died in 1879 at the age of thirty-nine. "The American Skating King," reads the inscription on the stone over his grave.

Louis Rubenstein, a Canadian, a pupil of Haines',

Skaters of a century or so ago often wore lavish costumes, primitive skates.

was the first noted figure skater on the American continent. He held the Canadian figure skating championship from 1878 until 1889; he won the American title in 1888 and 1889; and he journeyed to Russia in 1890 where he defeated the greatest European skaters of the day in open competition.

Up until the 1930s, the most prominent skaters were invariably amateurs. But this changed with Sonja Henie, the "Norwegian doll." In 1924 at the age of ten, she won the figure skating championship of her native Norway, and followed with the winning of ten world titles and three Olympic gold medals. But Miss Henie achieved her greatest fame as a professional, touring the United States in one ice show after another. Enormous crowds flocked to see her perform.

Since then, many other Olympic champions have followed the course set by Miss Henie, including Canada's Barbara Ann Scott, a gold medalist in 1948; America's Dick Button, Olympic champion in 1948 and 1952; Peggy Fleming, women's Olympic champion in 1968, and Dorothy Hamill in 1976. Miss Fleming also became well known as a featured performer on television ice shows.

Skating is one of the few activities that continues to be acclaimed as an art, a sport, and recreational activity. "The one thing that has remained constant for me," Dick Button once wrote, "through competition, professional performances, and long hours of practice, is the sheer joy I feel from skating." Many millions would agree.

GLOSSARY

BACK INSIDE EDGE—A curve made while the skater is traveling backward, the inside edge of the blade in contact with the ice.

BACK OUTSIDE EDGE—A curve made while the skater is traveling backward, the outside edge of the blade in contact with the ice.

BLADE—The hollow-edged length of steel mounted to the skate bottom upon which the skater travels.

BUNNY HOP—A jump from the flat of the blade, with the skater vaulting into the air from one skate, touching down on the toe picks of the other, and landing on the flat of the blade of the starting foot.

CROSSOVER—A turn executed by repeatedly crossing the free (or outside) skate around and in front of the other.

EDGE—Either one of the two opposing sides of the skate blade which are in contact with the ice; also, the curve that results when a moving blade edge cuts into the ice.

FIGURE—A design or pattern traced upon the ice. Most figures recognized by the USFSA are based upon the figure 8.

FIGURE SKATING—A type of skating in which prescribed geometrical designs, based on the figure 8, are traced upon the ice, and which also includes free skating, pair skating, and ice dancing.

FLAT—The noncurving section of a skate blade.

FORWARD INSIDE EDGE—The curve made when the skate travels forward, the inside edge of the blade in contact with the ice.

FORWARD OUTSIDE EDGE—The curve made while the skater is traveling forward, the outside edge of the blade in contact with the ice.

FREE SIDE—The side of the body above the skate that is off the ice; opposed to "skating side."

GLIDE—To move forward or backward on the blades.

HOCKEY STOP—A stop executed from a glide in which both blades are turned abruptly at right angles to line of travel.

ICE DANCING—Ballroom dancing to music on the ice surface.

INSIDE EDGE—The edge of the blade that runs along the arch side of the foot.

LONG AXIS—In the figure 8, an imaginary line through the midpoints of both circles which serves to divide the figure in half.

MOUNTING—Fixing the skate to the boot.

NEUTRAL POSITION—In stroking, when the shoulders and hips are square to the skater's line of travel.

OUTSIDE EDGE—The edge of the blade that runs along the outer side of the foot.

PAIR SKATING—A branch of figure skating in which two skaters execute various lifts, spins, and "free" movements simultaneously.

PATCH—A space on the ice rented to a skater to practice figures.

PATCH MARKER—In practicing figures, a device used to inscribe circles, axes, or loops upon the ice.

PIVOT—A movement in which the skater places the toe pick of one skate on the ice and circles around it.

PUSH OFF—To thrust forward or back on blade edge.

RADIUS—The front-to-back curve of a figure blade.

SCULLING—A beginner's exercise in which the skater moves either forward or backward by repeated in-and-out movements of the skates.

SHORT AXIS—In the figure 8, an imaginary line through the intersecting point of the two circles and at right angles to the long axis.

SKATING SIDE—The side of the body above the blade on which the skater is riding; opposed to "free side."

SNOWPLOW STOP—A beginner's stop in which both toes are turned inward, causing the blades to skid, halting the skater's forward movement.

SPIRAL—An unbroken series of circular glides skated on a blade edge.

STANCHIONS—The two verticle members of the blade which serve to connect the blade proper with the toe and heel plates.

STROKE, STROKING—Skating in the prescribed manner by coordinating a thrust, knee bend, and weight shift from one blade to the other.

T-STOP—A braking maneuver in which one skate is placed at right angles to the other.

TAKEOFF—The beginning of a jump.

THREE-TURN—A change in direction from forward to backward (or backward to forward) on the same foot. In executing the turn, a 3 pattern is traced upon the ice.

TOE PICKS—The several sharp projections at the front of the figure blade, which are used to grip the ice in certain spins and jumps; also called toe rakes.

TRACING—The line etched into the ice by a blade edge.

WALTZ JUMP—A jump in which the skater takes off from a forward outside edge, executes a half turn in the air, and lands on the back outside edge of the other skate.